Women's Studies Chronicles

Eloise Klein Healy

Laguna Poets Series # 99
at
The Inevitable Press

Women's Studies Chronicles

Copyright © 1998 by Eloise Klein Healy

Manufactured in the United States of America

at

The Inevitable Press
P.O. Box 249
Laguna Beach, CA 92652

Phone: (949) 494-6649

ISBN 1-891281-33-X

The **Laguna Poets Series** presents the work of readers featured in our Friday night programs at Laguna in a limited edition chapbook format. We are indeed pleased and honored that **Eloise Klein Healy**'s *Women's Studies Chronicles* are our Ninety-ninth issue .

Contents

INTRO TO WOMEN'S STUDIES

They sit like a grove of saplings or young angels,
unmindful of how their faces are open to me,
how every line so lightly carving their brows
is familiar, how their eyes betray what they are hiding
from me, from each other, themselves,
even the walls of the room.

Strewn in chairs or at attention, they wait,
hoping to add the class, maybe willing to behave
and sit like proper domesticated animals,
read all the books and turn in papers with no excuses.

This power to give life or take it
is what the avenging goddess must have felt,
but for me it's reduced now to
giving credit.

The young women hold everything in check,
the men measure me and before
the week is out, one or two will offer up
reductively sexist statements
to see if the hair on my spine will stiffen.
Yes, and then I will also bite, maul, tell the truth
and tell it in terms they know.

The avenging goddess must have welcomed
the same kinds of offerings—the great pile of shredded
animals burned to Artemis, bulls and goats torn
limb from limb and hanging on the ceremonial trees.
Yes, that goddess understood how far
the knife must go, the sacrifice must hurt,
to change the world.

I say to the women
        you will have powerful feelings,
        will fight with parents and boyfriends,
        will remember you have been raped or abused,
        will have to move away from home,
        maybe quit your job, change everything
        you believe   and admit to terror, fear
        of failure, anger, rage, fury, blind hate,
        and the blood curdling infinite and unrelenting
        knowledge of betrayal and lies, double dealings,
        humiliations, and the ignominious self-sacrificing
        you are expected to offer up daily
        because in that bloodly expulsion from the womb,
        at the moment you leapt into life,
        into the body of this world,
        you came born as female.

RECURRING DREAMS

Every time I lecture
on women and men,
I walk
through my fear.
I take
my sudden giddiness
as a sign of entry
or passage through
unknown dark words
spoken who knows when.

> *Don't*
> *talk against*
> *the men, don't*
> *let them know you*
> *know,*

> *or they*
> *will kill you,*
> *cut out your tongue,*
> *rape*
> *and burn*
> *your body, scatter*

your ashes, bones, soul.

They will deny your power
to know yourself
or to recognize in them
their fear, their dream of failure,
the fire that will not light,
the tinder steeped in blood.

SPEAKING THE TRUTH

From her desk, the young woman watches me
with this question in her eyes—

> *If I believe you, will I be crazy?*
> *Will I be as crazy as you sound to me*
> *and so convinced of the truth*
> *of your truth*
>
> *that I will turn to my own father*
> *and force his jaw open*
> *squeezing the round muscles*
> *with my thumbs and forefingers*
> *until the skin reddens from the force*
> *and the mandible threatens*
> *to collapse in ash,*
>
> *that I will turn to my mother*
> *and say, "no, there is no flame*
> *to burn me unless it is the flame*
> *of the lie, the endlessly fed flame*
> *of fear ?"*

2

In our next chapter, when this young woman learns why
Joan of Arc died—
  the real story
  behind the George Bernard Shaw theatrics
  girls recite at high school drama festivals,
  the real story behind the Church's fiction
  about her heresy—
that Joan burned
because she refused to give up
dressing in men's clothing,

then I'll light the question
behind another story behind the official scripts:

the actress Jean Seberg
with her shorn head
and radical racial/sexual politics—
the white star, a black man.

The beautiful actress
who played Joan,
had politics
too early for her time—
A black lover, a white star.

She was cloaked by the FBI with innuendos
of communist connections,
made an object lesson for her
so-called bohemian dereliction
of propriety.

Photos show her half-naked with a black man
lounging on a bed smoking.
(very Parisian, very unamerican).

She was labeled sexually possessed
instead of free.

Because it was made out she was crazy,
it was easy to believe
the circumstances of her demise
suited her—
she was found in a parked car
four days after her death,
the front and back seats
filled with trash.

STUDENT EVALUATION OF INTRO TO WOMEN'S STUDIES

(a found poem)

Intro to WS is a great place
to meet women.

I learned a lot.

I used to just look
at girl's breasts,
but women are really smarter
than I thought
since I've been talking to them.

DINING IN WITH HOMOPHOBIC LESBIANS

I will carry into all my days last night's scenario—
the cathedral-ceiling dining room,
the over-sized and over-stuffed furnishings,
the fantastical and absurd imitation flowers
of the homophobic lesbians
we had dinner with last night.

I will carry the rage and the sorrow
that sent us home early
through a lightning storm, the freeway
so drowned in water all the cars
had left their lanes and were ahead,
around, and behind us like a pack of animals
running wild.

It was a relief to escape those women
who dismissed young dykes
as girls who look like boys,
who all night called women *girls* or *ladies*,
who pronounced the word *feminist*
as some men do—
meaning unwashed and ugly females.

What work it was to eat at their table,
push food around the plate while trying
to move the mountain of hate
whose shadow they live in

with its plants more maniacal
than the ones in tortuous display
all around the rooms.

They live hidden in a wealthy isolation
more unstable than the foundations
of the expensively redone patio
perched on the edge of a cliff,
more twisted at the root
than the trees on their hillside
grasping for a footing after the rains.

And if the religious fanatics
come again for the lesbians,
it won't matter that these ladies
get their nails done weekly
or that their hair is perfectly Palm Springs
sand-dune sun-streaked.

These girls suck cunt the same as girl-boys
in Long Beach bars or dykes on bikes in Gay Pride parades,
and they'll go up in smoke the same,
and down in ash the same,
and have the same name,
the same shame, the same blame
for playing their kind of the lesbian game.

THE RAPE VICTIM'S NEWEST BOYFRIEND

framed himself in the doorway
big, blond,
would like to think
he's handsome.

His first office visit
he opined I didn't like men, did I?
Was I, he leaned in
until his chest broke the plane
between us,

married?

So that I got the whole picture,
he put his forearms on my desk
like lumber and complained.

Next visit, he checked the hall before entering.
Just a question he thought I could answer.
His new girlfriend some months earlier
had been raped.

Just what was wrong now
he couldn't say.
She was edgy and grey,
she was failing to weigh
her chances with him, in fact,
she didn't trust any men,
even him.

Voice and tone annoyed,
face conflicted and amazed, eyes not
in agreement with the rest, in fact,
the test was the eyes gauging if I'd engage.

Tell me (he licked his lips) why
she closes up when I touch her.
I only tickle—not much—
it's just a game
to hold her on the couch
and have some fun.

My gaze ripped free
from his eyes' flat stare
The air was clear
and I leaned back in my chair.
Then all the objects in the room disappeared.
The ground lay flat around me, mountains
ringing the scene and my muscles started to sing
the killing song.

"Get the hell out of here, you fucking asshole,"
I said, and realized with two doors
between me and the hall,
no one would ever hear my call for help.

But he grinned, took his book and left,
then dropped the course the same day.

ASKING FOR AN INCOMPLETE

Please, she says, now I am sitting
in the courtroom to make my homework.

I can only make it in handwriting
while I am waiting in the courtroom

to see if my husband will take
my children. Please, I am not

a bad mother. I am not a bad student.
After ten p.m. at the shelter

they say no more reading, no more
writing. Turn in any writing

to the court. Maybe, they say,
I cannot finish this class.

Please, I am not a bad mother.
I must keep my children from him.

///

The holes where my eyes should be meet the holes
where her eyes should be (Greek statues, pre-classical period,
empty dark orbs where semiprecious stones once were set
by hand), and we are not at my eighth floor office door but grip-
ping each other's arms in the courtyard as the men swarm over
the wall 900 BCE, each with the face of my colleague
in ST806 who has been looking disgustedly at the woman
crying, who watches my naked arm shielding her back,
my free hand smoothing her flying hair.

THE TEST

I

My students bend intently
over their desks, the test questions swirling
around their heads, the answers gathering
or slipping away.

I have taken them to the wall
in *The Handmaid's Tale*
where Margaret Atwood hung the bleeding bodies.
I have taken them there and forced them to touch
the red-brown O's of mouths now silenced.

I have held in front of them the photos
of the Triangle Shirt Waist Factory girls
flying through the air, unnecessary angels.
I have held the photos before them
like a Veronica holding the sweated and bloody
face of the Christ printed on her scarf.

Touch these wings, I demand.
Touch the concrete before these women
smash against it like bags of groceries
you'd spill going into your house—
they are full of life, not bread and wine.

II

My students bend over their tests
intent on making the right responses.
It is required to test them this way
but I would rather send them
in the patrol car to the frat house
with directions to write up the rape.
Touch the semen up a co-ed's ass.
How many kinds of semen are there?
And let us count the ways it gets around.

Here, I say, here is a wound
to compare and contrast to no other.
Here is a little piece of culture
on a swab. Look under the microscope
and see this culture growing
like a scream in this dish.

This red mouth, this is culture's test
of manhood, of womanhood,
and this outrage I force into essay form
so you can write out
what we really know.

THE WAY I FEEL COULD RUIN MY CAREER

California State University Northridge 1980-1991

The elevator spits me out,
one book bag almost dripping blood,
the other showing signs
of a struggle.

I'm off to a meeting
in the person of the lesbian poet
who runs a program in Women's Studies
in a state institution
of higher education, directing
my eyes to the dirty lineoleum
the government buys by the square mile
to pave the angular and lonely halls.

No relief on the walls or out a window,
a campus designed by committee
from plans drawn by lot.

Silly me, I asked one time
why we couldn't hang student artwork
in the halls.

"It agitates them
and between-class traffic
won't flow.
They don't come from backgrounds
where real art is part
of daily experience"

I X'd out my suggestion,
closed my notepad cover
and walked into the public world
chastened by a Dean—what does it mean
that I crave beauty?
What does it mean
I think they crave it, too?

What does it mean
to crave beauty and knowledge
in the same building?

The deans kept telling me
What they're here for is a degree,
but what I heard was:

"You wouldn't want to stimulate
impossible desires

You wouldn't want them to hear songs
they couldn't turn off.

You wouldn't want anything
to take these sterile buildings
to the ground,
now would you?"

•••••

Note: On January 17, 1994, a major earthquake struck Southern Cali-
fornia and destroyed many buildings on the CSUN campus, including
the one in which this poem had its origin. Although the quake was
centered in Reseda, it was named the Northridge Quake.

f/m

1

when I think the words *feminine/masculine*
my whole system goes into berserk everything I am about
traumatizing at the intersection of the words

then there's the slash in between.
I must cut myself/be cut into pieces—

the big gender fork coming out of the sky
impales me on the tines and cuts me like a lambchop

I am of course speaking as a woman
I am of course known as a woman
who would see things this way.

2

cut

cunt

count the number of times

country of origin unspecified island off the coast

3

fixed/moving
father/mother
fern/marble

4

I can't stand the splitting which privileges one side of the equation. I always knew algebra had the same kind of lie in it—that quality could be stripped from quantity. The desirable **X** can stand for anything. The completely possible substitute in any scheme. Is this straying from the topic or rather can I make it clear what the issue is here? The masculine is the magic **X** that can be anything anywhere while the feminine is **x**'d out in most equations.

 I will take on the task, therefore, of speaking for **xx**, the female who wants to formally claim what gets to be masculine, namely: the better clothes, the most comfortable shoes, baggy pants, overpoweringly sexual cologne, great cotton everything. All the things I paid a terrible price for in the days before androgyny.

And it goes without saying—political power

TO PETER IN GERMANY

1

Dear Peter,

I met three women this summer at Mono Lake. I knew they were foreigners because of their haircuts. I thought two of them might be dykes, and sure enough, they were East German lesbians. They had left their lovers at home while they were here doing research at the University of Oklahoma. I commented on what an out-of-the-way place they'd been sent to—like Oklahoma isn't exactly AMERICA—power center and all, but they thought they had seen the heartland. They were returning home to an uncertain future. What they said was their jobs weren't safe when men need to be employed—that's what they believed. I could only sympathize and pet their dog. In Berlin the wall may have fallen, but it fell on the women. No female faces rose in the wave of grey suits on the tide of democratic revolution.

2

Homegrown atrocities
surround me when
I look at the women
who come to sign up for classes—
the tight smile of one

whose body
is a coin rubbed
between her boss' fingers,
the unlined, unlearned face
of a local beauty,
spent by 23.

Deferential,
they sit
in front of
my desk,
apologetic

as a season
out of season,
to say, *"it's just a feeling,
I've never read anything."*

3

The dangers to my gender
are catalogued in the names
of foundations and social service agencies:
Haven House Shelter for Battered Women,
Alcoholism Center For Women, House
of Ruth, Sojourner, Lesbian Rights
Advocates, Beyond Survival.

The list goes on.

4

Dear Peter,

The effects you've seen of the Final Solution, built there in a landscape and historical moment, I give you. I honor the truth of the historical moment. When you come home to this city, when you come back to your friends and your place in our history, I can only say I won't know who I am to you or any man anymore. I speak out of the dead mouths now, I speak out of my terror for the history of women as it comes before us in living color and not as the dumb-show lie factory production which our common culture drags out in moth-eaten costumes; and while the tapdancing goes on, backstage is clitoridectomy, infibulation, genocidal rape. The meter is running, Peter—more women then Jews. Believe me, the sorry truth is more women than Jews. More women than Jews even. Hatred unto hatred. More. More. More than we can count.

5

Dirty fingers.
It begins and ends
with dirty fingers. The priests can burn
all the incense in the world,
cut up all the sacrificial chickens
and throw blood on the walls, chant the laws
of eternity and not one thin

red running down white
trickle of it
matters to me.

In my lifetime,
even with forty years of feminism,
cutting the sexual parts out of girls
can still be practiced in the name of religion
and culture.

Want to answer the question of what "eye for an eye"
I am talking about here?
Want to know why the revolution is still an itch
in my palm, why I lose
whatever civilizing effects culture
used to have on me?

All the non-violence in the world
has not saved female bodies
from men
and their lies:
theology-lie, philosophy-lie,
regulation-lie, history-lie,

lie lie lie lie lie.

I grant no one the benefit of the doubt
I speak their language now,
an eye for an eye, a part for a part.

I commit myself to kill
the pain
and what causes pain.
I commit myself
to the end of their world.

6

Dear Peter,

If a jawbone is found in the desert
separated from the body,
what's your guess, my friend?

Is it a woman?

Is it a habit?

Is it the natural law?